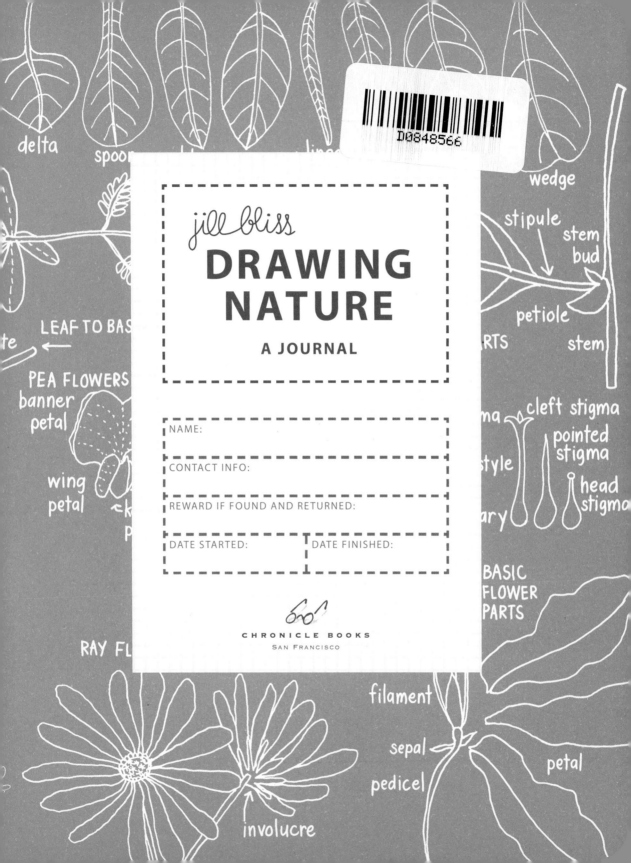

jill bliss

DRAWING NATURE

A JOURNAL

NAME:

CONTACT INFO:

REWARD IF FOUND AND RETURNED:

DATE STARTED: DATE FINISHED:

CHRONICLE BOOKS
SAN FRANCISCO

delta
spoon
linea
wedge
stipule
stem bud
petiole
stem
LEAF TO BAS
PARTS
PEA FLOWERS
banner petal
cleft stigma
pointed stigma
head stigma
style
wing petal
ary
BASIC FLOWER PARTS
RAY FL
filament
sepal
pedicel
petal
involucre

ISBN: 978-0-8118-7768-8

Manufactured in China

Design and illustrations by Jill Bliss
Typeset in Myriad

10 9 8 7 6 5 4 3 2 1

Chronicle Books LLC
680 Second Street
San Francisco, CA 94107
www.chroniclebooks.com

Many thanks to all my teachers and students throughout the years,
with special acknowledgment to the original Summer Sunday
Drawing Workshop attendees [Lauren, Gretchen, April, Angela,
Ben, Meredith, Kari, Ellen, Wendy, Liz, Annie, Linnea, Chrissy,
Susan, Rachel], and my team at Chronicle Books [Kim, Christina,
Becca, Kristen, and Yolanda].

for **LUCY**, my daily
nature co-observer

TABLE OF CONTENTS

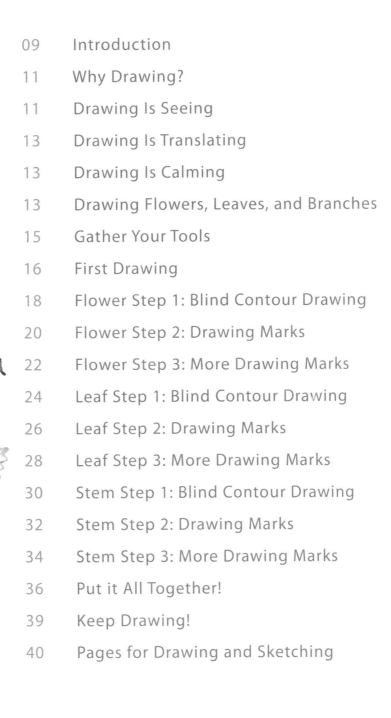

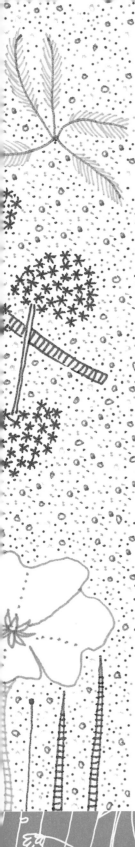

INTRODUCTION

During my formative years on a farm in Northern California, I spent hours every day romping around orchards and fields, closely inspecting the plants and animals around me. At an early age, I grew to appreciate the natural cycles of life, and the deep commitment every component within each cycle must have in order for everything to function properly. I constantly drew many of the things I encountered, and created entire illustrated worlds of interconnected communities.

In later years, I went to art school in New York City. It was there, amid the audible and visual noise of the "concrete jungle," that I realized the similarities between natural rural environments and manmade urban environments. Each has its own inherent order, and everything within each environment cultivates its own niche. For example, in the city you may find the old man who sits on his stoop each day to watch the world go by, while in a rural environment you have the old oak tree that does pretty much the same thing.

After five years in New York, I was homesick for the trees, flowers, and greenery of my childhood and relocated to San Francisco. It was there, in the verdant Presidio National Park, that I began teaching myself the names and anatomy of native flowers and plants by drawing them. Sitting next to a plant and observing all the little details that made it unique, I was mesmerized by the process of deep concentration—just sitting still, and enjoying the simple pleasures of the sun, the wind, and the ground beneath me.

Now that I look back on it, my life and work have been a natural progression. Making and drawing things is what I've always done with my free time, so I feel really lucky to be able to dedicate a lot of time and energy toward something about which I feel so passionate. I especially enjoy teaching and sharing my discoveries with others. This book stems from the Summer Sunday Drawing Nature Workshops that I lead every summer in the parks of Portland, Oregon, where I now live.

After going through the series of exercises in this journal, you'll gain "new eyes" to notice the minutiae and beauty in the natural world—and everything else around you. Even the most simple object can become complex the more you study it, and, conversely, complex objects can be simplified. In the first part of this journal, you'll learn tips and tricks for seeing and translating both seemingly simple and complex objects into marks on a page. Follow the exercises in sequence, as they serve as building blocks as you begin to draw. Then you can use the sketching pages in the latter half of the journal to practice what you've learned.

I hope this journal will help you experience the world in a whole new way—by drawing it! Drawing something encourages you to slow down, and to appreciate unnoticed details. It can be a meditative and rewarding experience.

WHY DRAWING?

When you get right down to it, drawing is a basic tool we humans have used to communicate with one another for a very long time. Think of ancient cave paintings, carved wood, stone pieces, or painted pottery. Some philosophers, including Vilém Flusser, believe drawing predates language as a primary communication tool, and that language was created as a way to further explain drawings.

Even now, in the Internet age where information can move around the world in seconds, we're discovering that many ideas are better expressed with images and diagrams rather than written language. Drawing is once again becoming a primary, ancient-yet-new tool we can use to communicate with others in our immediate physical environment, as well as in our online shared-interest communities made up of people throughout the world.

Exploring these shared communal interests, we're naturally led to observe the world around us with newly awakened eyes. In the process, we're rediscovering handcrafts, as well as drawing itself, as a way to reconnect and make personal marks in and about the world around us.

It's an exciting time to be a visual thinker!

DRAWING IS SEEING

Seeing and drawing are intertwined. Every person who can see has the capability to draw—it's just a matter of having a positive attitude, developing your seeing and drawing habits, and practicing on a regular basis.

In order to draw effectively, you need to accurately understand and record what you observe, to re-learn what you actually see in front of you, rather than perceiving the shorthand object your brain has learned to see after years of education. While these learned "seeing shortcuts" allow all of us a common ground to communicate, the secret of drawing is to be aware of this phenomenon and learn to look beyond it. For example, we all have a basic idea of what a flower looks like—a circle with four or five U-shaped petals around it. But if you take the time to look closely at a few specific flowers, the reality of the astounding variety of flower shapes becomes apparent. We all see differently—visually and emotionally—based on our unique life experiences. This journal will help you learn to "re-see" the world as you did when you were a child.

DRAWING IS TRANSLATING

Drawing is translating what you see into marks on a page to show others your unique way of seeing the world around you. Just like when you learned verbal language, you'll need to learn your own distinct visual vocabulary by trying out several different ones until you find one that works for you. Each of us has an exceptional, individual way of experiencing and translating the repeating patterns within the objects we encounter.

DRAWING IS CALMING

Drawing is about slowing down; it's a form of deep looking, a form of meditation. Like journaling, photography, and other art forms, drawing is something you can do every day as a way to explore your surroundings and your response to them. Doing something mindfully on a daily basis allows you to get out of your everyday routine, relax, and recharge. There are no boring subjects to draw! Keep an open mind and you will find something interesting to draw in everything you encounter.

DRAWING FLOWERS, LEAVES, AND BRANCHES

All organic forms, such as flowers, plants, trees, and rocks, are pretty forgiving for drawers of all skill levels. No one experiencing your drawing will know exactly what the flower or leaf you're depicting actually looked like, so you don't have to worry about faithful reproduction. This gives you license to explore, embellish, or simplify.

Flowers and leaves especially are a great place to begin your drawing practice because most consist of easy repeating forms. Once you learn how to see and draw one petal or leaf, you have the elemental knowledge to draw them all. And once you have that basic form down, it's easy to experiment with variations to give your drawing visual interest.

Begin by mentally breaking down the entire plant into its different parts and shapes: flower, leaf, and stem. Multiply and repeat, and soon you have a whole plant!

Ready to see and draw? Turn the page!

GATHER YOUR TOOLS

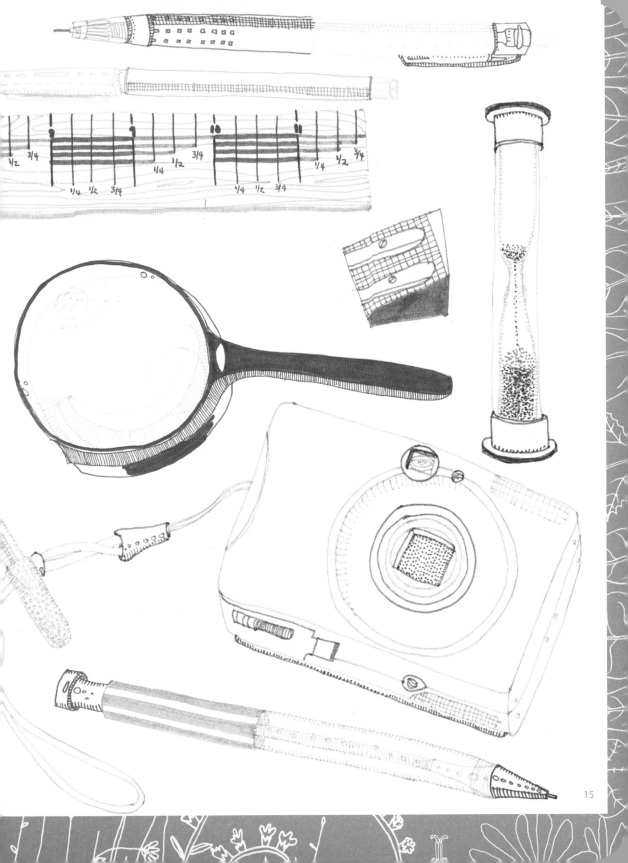

1/2 3/4 1/4 1/2 3/4 1/4 1/2 3/4 1/4 1/2 3/4

1/4 1/2 3/4 1/4 1/2 3/4

FIRST DRAWING

Sit outside on a lawn, in a yard, or a park, on the side of a hiking trail, or even inside at your favorite table or chair. Wherever you are, find a simple flower or leaf to draw. A daisy or a clover leaf will work perfectly. Draw it. Don't worry about doing it "right" or "wrong," as this will be your baseline drawing to look back upon. Hopefully you'll marvel at how much more you see once you've completed this journal!

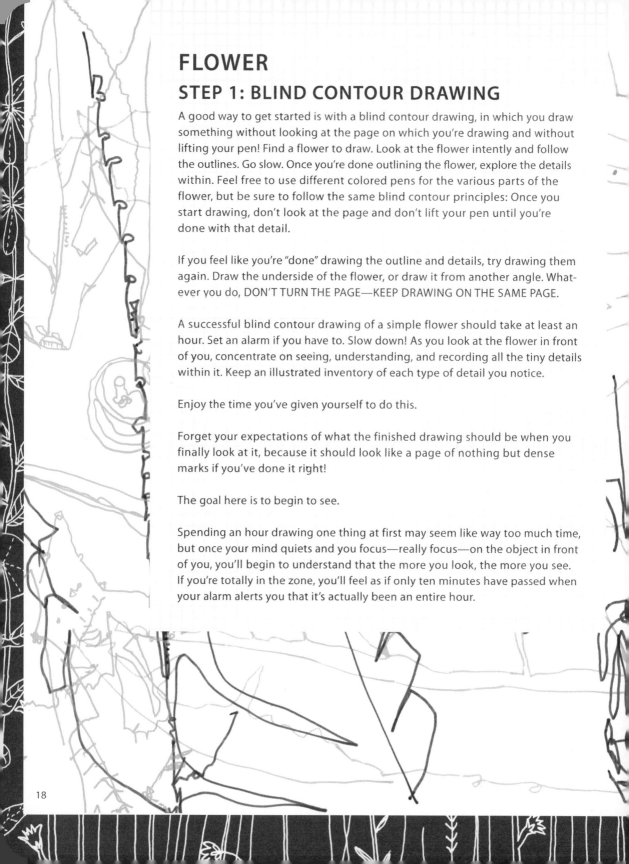

FLOWER
STEP 1: BLIND CONTOUR DRAWING

A good way to get started is with a blind contour drawing, in which you draw something without looking at the page on which you're drawing and without lifting your pen! Find a flower to draw. Look at the flower intently and follow the outlines. Go slow. Once you're done outlining the flower, explore the details within. Feel free to use different colored pens for the various parts of the flower, but be sure to follow the same blind contour principles: Once you start drawing, don't look at the page and don't lift your pen until you're done with that detail.

If you feel like you're "done" drawing the outline and details, try drawing them again. Draw the underside of the flower, or draw it from another angle. Whatever you do, DON'T TURN THE PAGE—KEEP DRAWING ON THE SAME PAGE.

A successful blind contour drawing of a simple flower should take at least an hour. Set an alarm if you have to. Slow down! As you look at the flower in front of you, concentrate on seeing, understanding, and recording all the tiny details within it. Keep an illustrated inventory of each type of detail you notice.

Enjoy the time you've given yourself to do this.

Forget your expectations of what the finished drawing should be when you finally look at it, because it should look like a page of nothing but dense marks if you've done it right!

The goal here is to begin to see.

Spending an hour drawing one thing at first may seem like way too much time, but once your mind quiets and you focus—really focus—on the object in front of you, you'll begin to understand that the more you look, the more you see. If you're totally in the zone, you'll feel as if only ten minutes have passed when your alarm alerts you that it's actually been an entire hour.

FLOWER
STEP 2: DRAWING MARKS

Get to know the marks that resonate with you! You are now free to look at the page and lift the pen as you draw. Note the different "flower types" shown on the back inside cover of this journal and keep in mind what type of flower you're drawing.

Draw your flower at least five different times, each time exploring it completely using only one type of mark per drawing. Some examples are shown on the left of this page for your inspiration.

The idea is to study the shapes and forms you see within your flower. You'll notice that some marks work better than others for certain parts.

You may have also noticed by now this little Nature Secret: Nature loves simple marks—lines, circles, dots—and organic uses of those marks. You'll never find perfectly straight lines or perfect right angles in natural objects. This gives you permission to experiment!

FLOWER
STEP 3: MORE DRAWING MARKS

Now draw your flower at least five different ways again, each time exploring it completely using SEVERAL types of marks per drawing. The marks on the left of this page may help inspire you.

The idea is to study the shapes and forms you see within your flower, and learn how to effectively use combinations of marks.

LEAF
STEP 1: BLIND CONTOUR DRAWING

Find a leaf and follow its outline without looking at the page on which you're drawing and without lifting your pen. When you're done with the outline, feel free to use different colors for other details of the leaf, but be sure to follow the same blind contour principles: Once you start drawing, don't look at the page and don't lift your pen until you're done with that part.

If you found it difficult in the last blind contour exercise to not look at the page as you drew your flower, try shielding the page with your free hand or another sheet of paper, or placing the journal in your lap under the table if you're seated.

If you feel like you're "done" drawing the outline, draw it again. Draw the under-side of the leaf, or draw the leaf from different angles. Whatever you do, DON'T TURN THE PAGE—KEEP DRAWING ON THE SAME PAGE.

Once again, a successful blind contour drawing of a simple leaf should take at least an hour. Set an alarm. Slow down and enjoy the time you've given yourself to do this! Appreciate the forms and keep an illustrated inventory of each type of detail you notice. Forget your expectations of what the finished drawing should look like, because it should look like a page of nothing but dense marks if you've done it right! The goal here is to begin to see, to break free of your expectations of what you think you see.

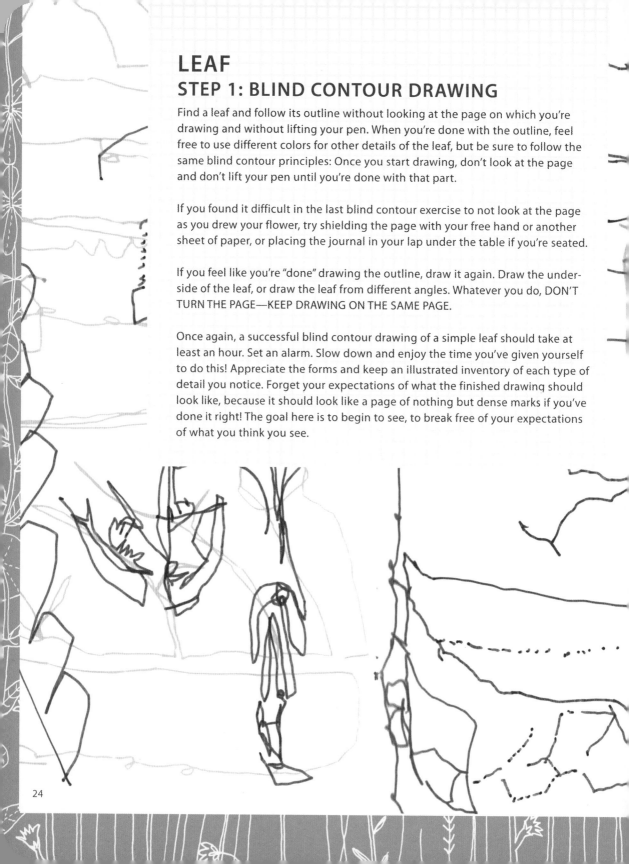

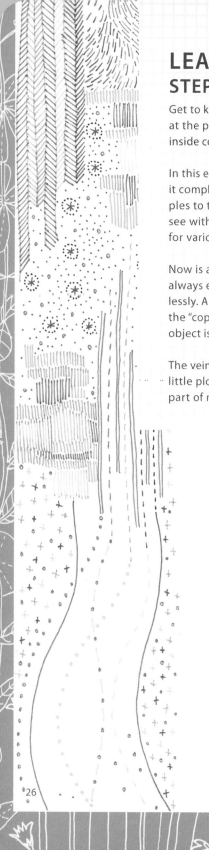

LEAF
STEP 2: DRAWING MARKS

Get to know the leafy marks that resonate with you! You are now free to look at the page as you draw. Note the different "leaf types" shown on the back inside cover of this journal and keep in mind what type of leaf you're drawing.

In this exercise, draw your leaf at least five different times, each time exploring it completely using only one type of mark per drawing. See some of my examples to the left for inspiration. The idea is to study the shapes and forms you see within your leaf. You'll notice that certain marks work better than others for various parts.

Now is a good time to let you in on another little Nature Secret: Nature is always economical, using the same simple shapes and repeating them endlessly. A natural form is made up of other, smaller repeated forms, similar to the "copy" and "paste" functions on your keyboard. Part of really looking at an object is uncovering and decoding the simple repeating patterns within it.

The veins in your leaf look like a road map, don't they? Or the boundaries of little plots of land. After all, people, and the way we organize things, are a part of nature, too!

LEAF
STEP 3: MORE DRAWING MARKS

Now draw your leaf at least five different ways again, each time exploring it completely using SEVERAL types of marks per drawing. I've drawn some marks at the margin of the page to serve as inspiration.

Get to know the shapes and forms within your leaf, and begin to learn how to effectively put together combinations of marks.

STEM
STEP 1: BLIND CONTOUR DRAWING

You know the drill by now: Find a stem and draw its outline with your pen. Don't look at the page while you draw and don't lift your pen! Once you're done with the outline of the stem, explore the details within it. Try using different colored pens, but be sure to follow the same blind contour principles: Don't look at the page and don't lift your pen until you're done with that detail. If you feel like you're "done" drawing, draw it again. Whatever you do, DON'T TURN THE PAGE—KEEP DRAWING ON THE SAME PAGE.

Remember: Go slow. A successful blind contour drawing of your stem should take at least an hour. As in the previous exercises, keep an illustrated inventory of each type of detail you notice—all the different lines and shapes that make up your stem. You'll find that your end result—a page of dense marks—will help you to see stems in a whole new way.

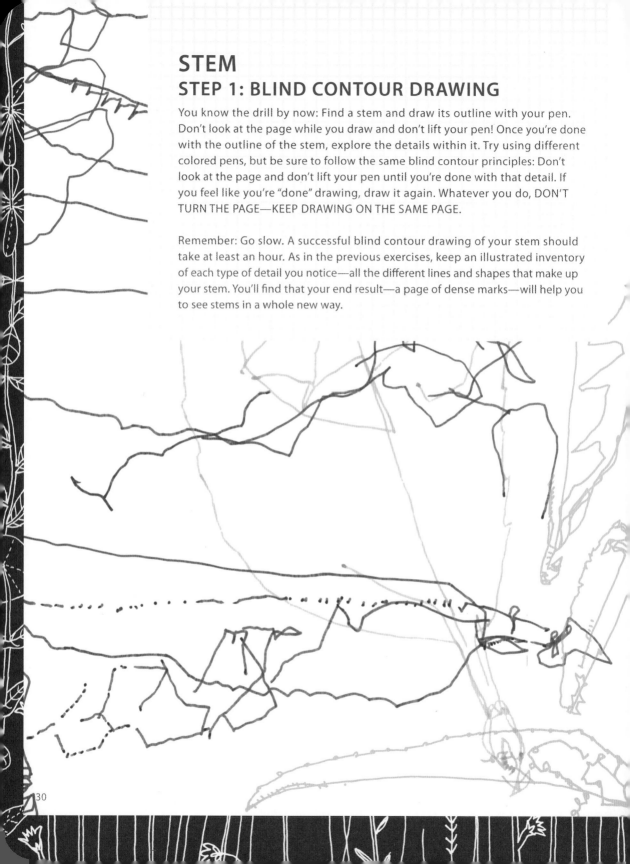

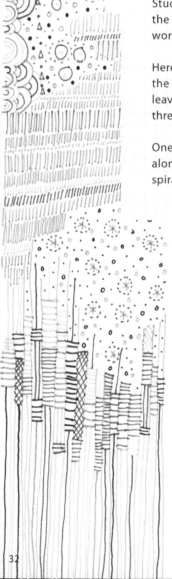

STEM
STEP 2: DRAWING MARKS

Get to know the marks that resonate with you! You are now free to look at the page as you draw. Note the different "stem types" shown on the back inside cover of this journal and keep in mind what type of stem you're drawing.

Draw your stem at least five different ways, each time exploring it completely using only one type of mark per drawing. Some examples shown on this page may inspire you.

Study the shapes and forms you see within your stem. Study and re-create the texture of the surface using your marks. You'll notice that some marks work better than others for certain parts.

Here's a Nature Secret for you: There is always a simple, reliable system within the seemingly complex structure of each natural object. Are the nodes or leaves on your stem symmetrically or asymmetrically placed? Repeated two, three, or five times?

One last Nature Secret: If you think the arrangement of the nodes or leaves along the stem are random, chances are they're not; they're on a spiral. The spiral is nature's favorite way to "randomly" organize itself.

STEM
STEP 3: MORE DRAWING MARKS

Now draw your stem once again at least five different times, each time exploring it completely using SEVERAL types of marks per drawing. There are some mark-making examples on the left.

Study the shapes and forms within your stem, and observe how various combinations of marks work together.

PUT IT ALL TOGETHER!

Okay, you've drawn an individual flower, leaf, and stem! Now you're ready to draw the entire plant and study the way each component connects!

The same basic natural drawing techniques and tips you've just learned apply to all other natural objects, so you should progress from drawing an entire plant to drawing an entire landscape.

Try it here!

KEEP DRAWING!

Before I let you loose, here are a few ideas on how to incorporate drawing and this journal into your daily life.

* Try using more than one color in your drawings. Start with two, then three, then four, then a full color palette!
* Try collaging found papers and images and drawing on top of them.
* Try different mark-making tools: crayons, pens, pencils, pastels, paint, sticks dipped in ink or paint, etc. Each has its own characteristics that affect the way you're able to depict an object!
* Promise yourself to draw at least one drawing a day, every day.
* Photograph or scan your daily drawings and post them online each day to encourage yourself to keep practicing.
* Start a weekly or monthly drawing club with your friends to encourage one another.

Don't worry, you won't be entirely alone—I've sprinkled the following pages with my own tips and drawings to encourage and remind you!
Ready to draw on your own? Turn the page. . . .

NOTES

Resist your temptation to turn the page on a mistake. Instead, keep working at it until you're happy with the results!

40

NOTES

There is no right or wrong way to record your observations. Want to incorporate writing, poetry, or a list? Use this note-taking space!

DATE | SUBJECT | LOCATION

NOTES | This is not a test. You will not be graded. You cannot fail.

DATE | SUBJECT | LOCATION

DATE	SUBJECT		LOCATION

Challenge yourself to work with only one color.
It will help you create a variety of different marks!

DATE | SUBJECT | LOCATION

NOTES

Draw an object that you think is boring or ugly. Find and depict its inner beauty here!

NOTES

Have a complicated item? Draw each part separately first, several times.
Once you understand each separate part, you can combine them together!

NOTES

Drawing is like handwriting: we each have our own unique and innate style and approach! Draw more to find yours!

DATE | SUBJECT | LOCATION

DATE | SUBJECT | LOCATION

NOTES

Try drawing small objects larger, or large objects smaller.
This is a good way to see the object differently.

DATE	SUBJECT	LOCATION

Frustrated with a particular drawing? Show it to someone else to gain a fresh perspective

NOTES

Choose a complicated object to draw, but simplify the shapes you see.
Break it down into a series of repeating simple forms.

NOTES

Draw the same object from 5 different angles in order to fully understand how the different shapes within it work together.

NOTES Give your object an imaginary story. Draw it according to the parameters of your story.

DATE   SUBJECT   LOCATION

DATE | SUBJECT | LOCATION

NOTES

In a drawing club? Trade halfway done drawings for a different perspective on the same object!

DATE   SUBJECT   LOCATION

Draw the same object five times, each time using only one type of mark. This will help you understand which marks work best for each part.

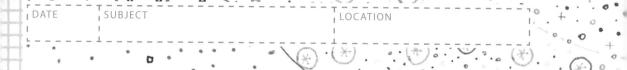

DATE | SUBJECT | LOCATION

Stop drawing long before you think you're done.
Challenge yourself to see the beauty in empty space!

Are you having a challenging day and losing your patience?
Give yourself five minutes to sit and draw something in front of you.

NOTES

Don't be afraid to draw in the style of someone else you admire.
By imitating someone else, you're exploring and finding your own style.

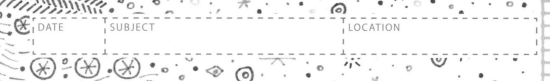

DATE | SUBJECT | LOCATION

Do you think your drawing isn't an accurate representation of your object? Turn the page and come back to it another day for another perspective.

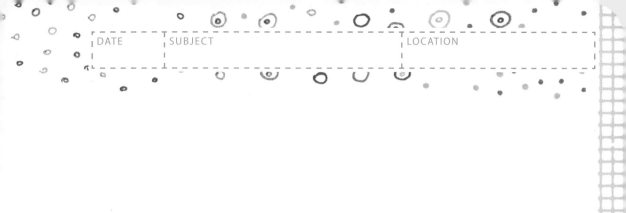

NOTES

Overwhelmed with the complexity you see before you? Draw one small part at a time and you'll be done before you know it!

Draw your object with one hand, and then the other hand. Look at the results. Are there big differences between each of these drawings?

NOTES

Set a timer and give yourself only thirty seconds to draw an object.
Then give yourself an hour to draw it. Which drawing suits you better?

NOTES

Remember that no one experiencing your drawing of an object will have the object in front of them with which to compare it.

NOTES

The difference between what you see and what you draw is your own uniqueness. No one else can see or draw exactly as you do! Celebrate that!

DATE	SUBJECT	LOCATION

NOTES

Break down an entire plant into its different parts: flower, leaf, stem. Multiply and repeat, and soon you'll have the whole plant!

Remember that all natural forms are made up of other smaller repeating forms. Part of seeing an object is decoding the simple forms within it.

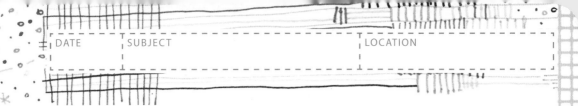

NOTES

Think you're done? Keep going! Don't be afraid to create a mess.
Remember that mistakes are opportunities to learn!

NOTES

Challenge yourself to draw using a color that isn't your favorite.
The results may surprise you!

NOTES | Explore the object in front of you, experiment with your marks!

NOTES

Forget your expectations. The difference between
faithful reproduction and your drawing is character.

NOTES

Remember that nature loves simple marks: lines, circles, dots. You never find perfectly straight lines or right angles in natural objects.

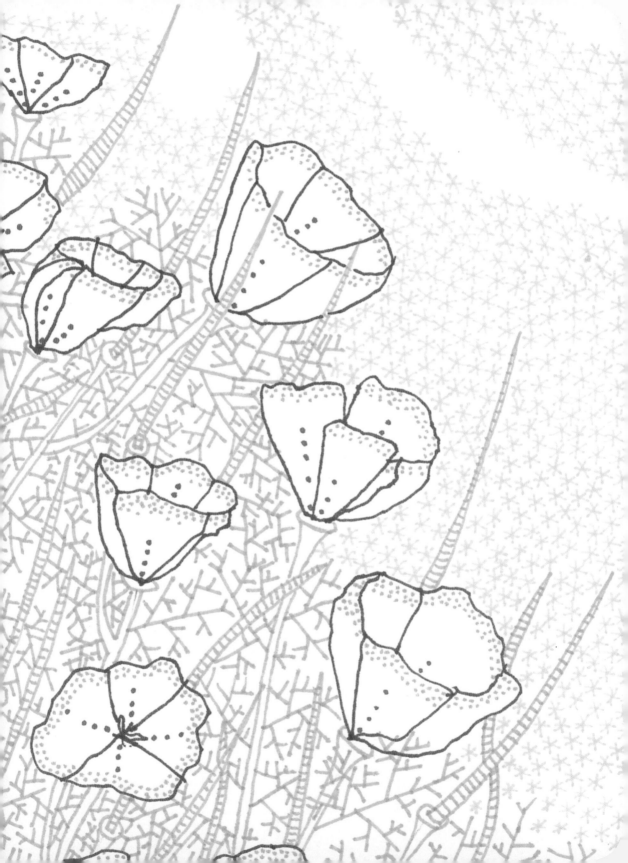

DATE   SUBJECT   LOCATION

Draw one object in front of you, then another object on the same page.
Create an environment for these two objects to live together.

DATE | SUBJECT | LOCATION

Does the object in front of you remind you of something else?
Explore that idea! Use it to uncover a whole new world within your object.

Can't make sense of how the marks on your object are organized? Chances are it's probably based on a spiral, nature's randomizer!

Have you been using only one type of mark-making tool? Try others! Each has its own characteristics that effect your depictions.

NOTES

To add personality to your drawings, exaggerate one of the details you see. Does the stem veer to the left a bit? Make it veer even more in your drawing.

DATE	SUBJECT	LOCATION

NOTES Don't be afraid to include written notes to yourself as you draw! These will be valuable reminders later.

DATE  SUBJECT LOCATION

Explore drawing the same object using a different color.
Does it change the depiction of the object?

Acquaint yourself with one small object in front of you. Then expand! Draw a dandelion, then the plant to which it's attached, then the surrounding plants.

NOTES

Drawing something you've drawn before? Review your past drawings for tips, strategies, and ways to improve your depiction this time.

DATE	SUBJECT	LOCATION

NOTES | Breathe calmly, draw slowly. Enjoy this time you've given yourself!

NOTES

Faced with an overwhelming object or scene, but determined to depict it?
Focus on depicting one small element first, then another, then another.

Not much time? Study and draw only the part
of the object you see that is most interesting to you.

NOTES

Relax, observe, and record what you see in front of you.
You haven't really seen something until you've drawn it.

NOTES

You don't have to be somewhere special in order to draw. Take a look around you right now for a plant or other natural object!

DATE	SUBJECT	LOCATION

NOTES

Not feeling inspired? Challenge yourself to draw the first thing you see.
Then draw something else you see. Make it special by drawing it!

DATE   SUBJECT   LOCATION

NOTES

Nature is not something that is somewhere else—it is all around you!
Explore your surroundings in these pages!

NOTES | There are so many forms within nature! Celebrate them all!

NOTES

Once you're finished with this page, you'll be able to experience this moment again and again.

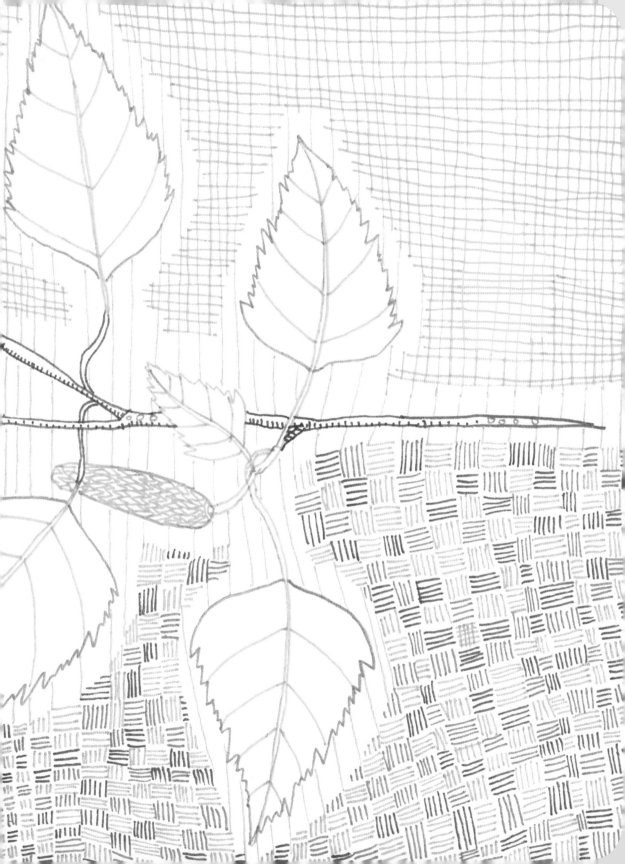

NOTES   Explore your own creativity, powers of observation, and mark-making.

By drawing, you are recording this moment for your future self to remember.

NOTES

It takes practice and a daily commitment to become a good observer and drawer.
Give yourself that daily gift!

NOTES

This journal, and your drawings within it, can be a useful tool for relaxing!

NOTES

In addition to drawing what's around you, collect objects during the course of the day to draw later!

Drawing not only helps you focus and reflect
on the world around you, but on yourself as well!

NOTES   Does your drawing feel as if it's lacking personality? Try doing a blind contour.

NOTES | The more you observe the world around you, the more you will know and understand it

Allow your mistakes to inspire you. Transform them into something new.

DATE	SUBJECT	LOCATION

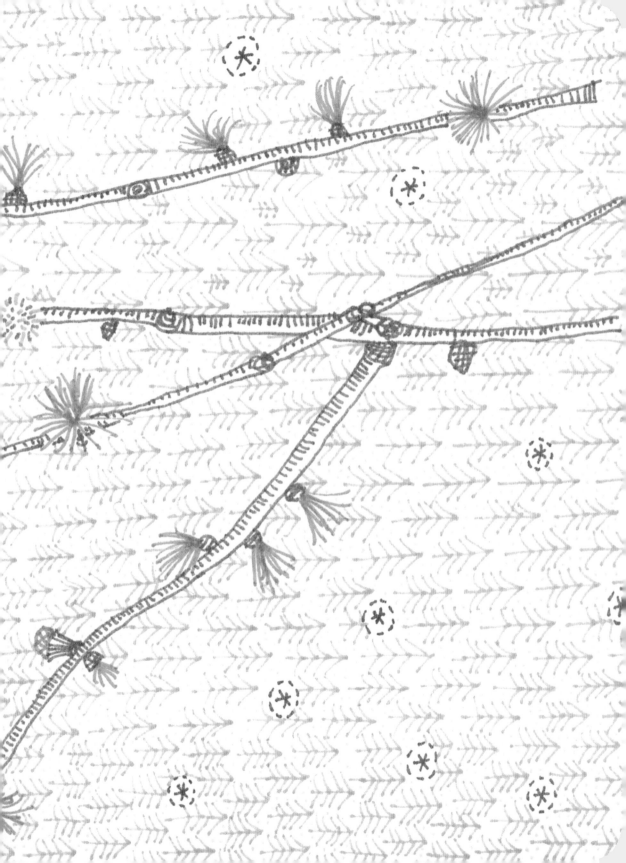

NOTES

Challenge yourself to work with two colors. Use the color combinations to create a variety of different marks!

NOTES — Draw an object that you think is beautiful. Find a new way to depict its beauty here.

DATE | SUBJECT | LOCATION

NOTES Have a complicated subject? Draw it as simply as you possibly can.

NOTES   Keep drawing every day!

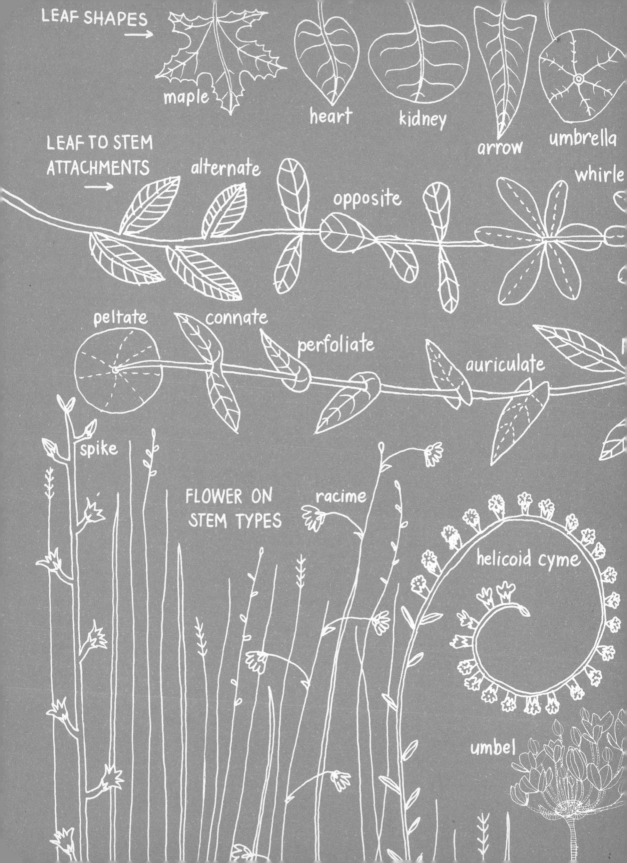

LEAF SHAPES →

maple

heart

kidney

arrow

umbrella

LEAF TO STEM ATTACHMENTS →

alternate

opposite

whirle

peltate

connate

perfoliate

auriculate

spike

FLOWER ON STEM TYPES

racime

helicoid cyme

umbel